Jan Bedel

and other Cornish Sayings

Collected by Kathleen Hawke

'Like Tommy Dumplens after guidize supper, car'
me home an' don't bend me, for I'm feeling rather
possed up'.

Tor Mark Press – Redruth

First published 1973 as 'Cornish Sayings, Superstitions and Remedies'
Published by Dyllansow Truran 1981.

This edition published 1998 by Tor Mark Press
United Downs Industrial Estate, St Day, Redruth, Cornwall TRl6 5HY,

@ 1998 Tor Mark Press: ISBN 0 85025 369 1

Cover illustration and line drawings by Jenny Williams.

Designed by Raymond Lancefield, The Design Field, Truro.

Printed in Cornwall by R. Booth (Bookbinder) Ltd & Troutbeck Press,
Antron Hill, Mabe, Penryn TRl0 9HH.

The TOR MARK series

FOLKLORE

Classic Cornish ghost stories
Classic Devon ghost stories
Classic ghost stories from the Land's End
Classic West Country ghost stories
Cornish fairies
Cornish folklore
Cornish legends

Customs and superstitions
Demons, ghosts and spectres
Devon customs
Devon legends
Folk tales from the Land's End
The pixy book

OTHER TITLES

Charlestown
China clay
Classic Cornish anecdotes
Cornish fishing industry
Cornish mining – at surface
Cornish mining– underground
Cornish mining industry
Cornish recipes
Cornish saints
Cornish smuggling industry
Cornwall in camera
Cornwall's engine houses
Cornwall's railways
Devonshire jokes and stories
Do you know Cornwall?
Down 'long weth we
Exploring Cornwall with your car
Fed fitty
Houses, castles and gardens
Introducing Cornwall

King Arthur – man or myth?
Lost ports of Cornwall
Old Cornwall – in pictures
The pasty book
Shipwrecks around Land's End
Shipwrecks around the Lizard
Shipwrecks – Falmouth to Looe
Shipwrecks – St Ives to Bude
Short Cornish dictionary
The story of the Cornish language
The story of St Ives
The story of Truro Cathedral
Strange tales of the Cornish coast
Tales of the Cornish fishermen
Tales of the Cornish miners
Tales of the Cornish smugglers
Tales of the Cornish wreckers
Twelve walks on the Lizard
What shall we do with the smuggled
    brandy?

As tough as Hancock's mother

Black as a tinker
Stinkin' as a polecat
Sick as a shag
Limp as a dish-rag or dish clout
Near as the grave
Tough as ole Sir Nick
Dear as saffron
Mazed as a curly [curlew]
Dry as a boot
Tough as Hancock's mother
Tired as a donkey
Rusty as an anchor
Black as a turf-rick toad
Full as an egg
As hardened as Pharaoh
As ragged as Jy weth es shirt hangin' out
Sick as a gurnet

*'Everybody do know what
to do with a kicking horse
except he that got un'.*

Rough as a downser [bullock on downs]
As light as a gay [broken china]
A pasty as long as Jan Bedella's fiddle
Stiff as a poss [post]
Dead as door nail
As smooth's a bulhorn [snail]
As smart as a half-scraped carrot
As handy's a showl
Hot as lead
As stupid as an owl
Thin as a griddle
As thin as a rushlight
As fat as a durgey [badger]
Cold as a quilkin [frog]
Wisht as a winnard [red wing]
Busy as batty, dawn't knaw which way to steer nor turn
Eyes as black as sloanes [sloes]
Happy as a duck
As wild as a fitcher [ferret]
Deef [deaf] as a haddick [haddock]
Wet as a shag [cormorant]
As awkward as a cow with a musket
As old as my little finger and a bit older than my teeth
As yellow as a keet's foot
Rough as a bear's paw
Dark as a dog's guts
Rough as a badger's back
Daft as a wagon 'oss
As heavy as tin
Vexed as fire
As stinkin' as fish
As yalla [yellow] as train [pilchard oil]
As pluffy as silk
Dark as a shaft
Small as a croggan
Taisy as a snake
Sour as a sab [common sorrel]

Plum as bun dough
Fullish as a wagon 'oss
Dry as a lime burner's shoe
As suant's a fiddle [smooth]
As pale as cloth
As green as a lick [leek]
As rotten as a pear
Deep as Dolcoath
Proud as Lucifer
Cold as Greenland
Fat as butter
Tough as ling
As cross as two sticks
Black as the devil's crowst bag [lunch bag]
Honest as the sun
Rusty as a handcart
As dry as a chip
Pleased as a cat with two tails
As thin as a willow rod
Thirsty as a gull
Looking as wise as a duck at a thunder cloud
As clumsy as a beddax [tool for digging]
As smart as a miller taking tolls
As sticky as a dough pan
As weak as a goose chick
Mazed as a brush or broom
As crooked as a thorn
As warm as a pie
As rough as a grater
As smooth as new milk
As blunt as a dag [miners axe]
Healthy as a trout
As drunk as a Piraner
As good as a Christmas play
Big as bull's beef
As plum as a wont pile [mole-hill]
Straight as a pound of candles [good character]

If there's any difference they're both alike

He looks as if a good meal's meat would do him good
Wan of Pharoah's lean kind
A back like a barn door
A back like a turf rick
Head like a turmot
Feet like hafe-crown shovels
Behind like a buttertub
Like two hellens clapped together [hellens = slates]
Like a bundle of straw tied in the middle [fat person]
Oal of a hog stog [in a muddle]
He couldn't stop a pig in a passage [bandy legged person]
Nobody will stop their horse from galloping to look at you
Rubbing through
   like the heel of a
   stocking
Like a yard of pump
   water [hair]
Rid round the gills
   [of a person
   crying]
Looking like a dying
   duck in a
   thunderstorm
Like Tregony band,
   three scats
   behind

*'He couldn't stop a
pig in a passage'.*

Warped up like a planchen
Steamin' like a crock
Staving along like a man going to a wreck
Proud in his own conceit, like Same Lidgey's chick
Like Ludlow's dog leaning agen the wall to bark
Like a gander geeking in a bussa [geeking means
    peeping and a bussa was an old earthenware
    salting pot – so an over curious person]
Off like a star-shot [in a hurry]
Fit like a stocking on a man's nose
Laikin' like a basket
Bossed about like stinking fish
Dressed to death like Sally Hatch
As knowing as Kate Mullet, and she was hanged for
    a fool
Like a tom-toddy [or totty], all head and no body
Outward flink, inward stink [flink=flash]
Looking like a tooth drawer
Face like a brandy bottle [red]
All behind like the cow's tail
Like Jan Lobb's eyes, hanging in lerrups [rags]
Looking like a stewed owl
Like an owl looking out of an ivy bush
Looking like a white-washed wall [pale person]
Blawed up like a wilkie [small toad]
All sixties and seventies [in a muddle]
She edn' bigger than three-happorth of pence
You wouldn't think butter would melt in her mouth
She's like a straight Jane from the workhouse
Like Lady Fan Todd, dressed to death and killed
    with fashion
Blawed up like a toad 'pon the dew
Blushing like a piny [paeony]
Like Nanny Paynter's hens, high upon legs
Dressed up like a lawyer
Wear pink to make the boys wink
Looking like a winnard [looking cold]

Oal of a dither

Backwards an' forwards like Boscastle Feer [Fair]
Grizzlin' like a badger gwain to faist
Scritchin' like a whitnick [weasel]
Like a bear weth a sore head
Too slow to carry cold dennar
Gwain like a long-dog
Shaking like a apsen leaf
Scrumped up like a hedgehog
Sweating like a poultice
Going sideways like a
    crab going to jail

'Happy on me awn
dung heap'.

You'd think she was brought up in Court, pigs one end and she
    t'other, [said of a proud person]
Always on the ran dan [never home]
Gwain like a 'oss in a 'arra [harrow]
Put in weth the bread an' took out weth tha cakes [deficient person]
Laughing like a pisky
Glazin' like a stat [stoat]
Like Farmer Hocking's ducks, more gab than guts
Busted up like a three-halfpenny chick on a wheaten arish [stubble]
    [after eating too much]

Live like fighting cocks [folk who live well]
Oal of a motion like a Mulfra toad on a rid hot shovel
Clunkin' like a toad [swallowing]
Like Jan Tresize's geese, never happy unless they be wheer they
    baint
You don't need that more than a toad needs side-pockets.
Going like Billy o' the grinder
Like a cat in a bunfire [bonfire]
Ballin' like a Benner Bull [Binnerton]
Grulling like a bear with a sore head
Happy on me awn dung-heap [contented person]
Glazin' like a stecked pig
Like Mawther's cloamen cat, hollow to his toes
Slept like a ringer
A temper like a fowl
Like a crab going to a christening [going sideways]
She never said bee nor baw [didn't reply]
She'll live and die in that old thing [favourite garment]
She's a proper whiz [unmanageable]
He's a proper limb [limb of the devil, unruly child]
Big above the shoulders [conceited]
She'll talk till the cows come home
Going to the goat's house to see for wool
Going like a lamplighter
She got brass enough to make a copper kettle
She'd skin a flea for a farthing
For pity's sake stop gulging, you'll chuck yerself [eating quickly;
    choke]
She's a proper wild-de-go [rash; reckless]
I forgot myself [went to sleep]
Worse than a flea to catch [never home]
Always on the randy [never home]
Like a toad under a harrow [weighed down]
Aw gate knaw nothing gwain nowheer [stupid person]
Always ill and sickly, more likely to live than die quickly
You'd think money grew upon fern [said of a spendthrift]
Take yer hands out yer pockets, they'll look like want catchers'
    pockets [want = mole]

'As awkward as a cow
with a musket'.

Deaf on one ear and can't hear on the other
She'll stick her stanning' ef she don't sell a happorth
He a bin awverlooked [illwished]
Can't tell a... from the track of a duck [stupid person]
If yiew wur ti diew as yiew oft to diew, yiew wud diew a gud deal
  better than yiew diew diew [North Cornwall]
Bit by bit as the cat said when he swallowed the hatchet, I'll manage
  it, but it'll be a tight fit
Don't knaw nuff to knaw they don't knaw nothing
Like some helpers, pulling down with a bar ire [iron] and propping
  up with a stocking needle

'Ow be knackin' fore? [How are you?]

Right as ninepence
Clemmed to the marra. [Marrow – feeling cold]
All awver alike like a Bryanite [answer to health enquiry]
In a proper boil [hot and bothered]
Running round like a scalded cat
Can't blaw nor strike [don't know which way to turn]
Like Tommy Dumplens after guldize supper, car' me home an' don't
    bend me, for I'm feeling rather possed up
My head don't save my heels. [forgetful person]
As thick as three in a bed
Strong in the arm, weak in the head
Like a fly in a jam pot [can't keep still]
The poor soul was in some taking. [upset]
Just between the driftwood and the hard wood. [just managing to
    keep going]
Between both, as Bucca said
Like death on mop-stick
Like Purser Hosking's mules – won't bear jesting
As dazed as a duck against thunder
Like a caage of bones (skeleton, very thin person)
As whisht (sickly) as a strange cat in a barnbold

'As thick as
three in a bed'.

Hearth and home – Happy on me awn dung heap

Will 'ee have a drop of warm? [a cup of tea]
Water bewitcht, tea begritcht [weak tea]
Tatie and point [point to the meat]
Put the wood in the hole [shut the door]
Packed in like herrings in a box
Sewed on with a red hot needle and burning thread [loose button]
Time to go up tembern hill [upstairs to bed]
Hung up his hat [said of a young man invited into supper by his lady
    love]

'Hung up his hat'.

Let the children race over nine lord's land
Where cobwebs are plentiful kisses are scarce
We don't pull and drag Sundays [shake mats]
It is often good manners to ask but not always take
He's a brave man that ate the first oyster
They never taste who always drink
Ever drunk ever dry
A slow drink is better than a dry sermon
They that make a hard bed for themselves must lie on it
A new broom sweeps clean, but an old one is good for corners

Take care you don't burn the malkin [A cloth for cleaning the oven –
    if burnt useless, so keep mum about your secret]
Lev'n go he's dry eating as the old man said of the hare
It's got a silver tail [a new thing]
Big 'nuff for Dr Boase
Uncle Will Ben's grace
    'God bless the meat and noe let's eat'
Hitched up [said of children not looked after]
They that can'y schemey must louster [if you can't plan you have to
    work the harder]
Opportunities like eggs come one at a time
Light suppers make long days
He that must thrive must rise at five

Good and bad luck at home
It is unlucky to burn egg shells
Sew on Saturday sew to the Devil; Saturday should be spent
    preparing for Sunday
Sew on Good Friday and you will prick the Saviour
Mending clothes on your person indicates a row
It is unlucky to put the bellows on the table
A kettle turned spout inwards indicates a storm at sea
It is unlucky to bring May blossom [hawthorn] or furze indoors [or
    blackthorn]

    Cut your nails on Monday for news [it could be bad news]
        On Tuesday for a new pair of shoes
        On Wednesday for a letter
        On Thursday for something better
        On Friday for sorrow
    On Saturday see your fair true love tomorrow
    On Sunday the Devil will be with you all the week

Never tell your dream before breakfast
It is unlucky to bring old iron into the house
You sweep your luck away if you sweep dust out through the
    doorway
If you put money outdoors on the window-sill on 31st December
    and bring it in on New Year's Day you will bring in money all the
    year

It is unlucky to open an umbrella indoors
If you wash clothes on Innocents' Day you wash one of the family away
Wash blankets in May and you wash one of the family away
It is lucky to pick up a pin with the head turned towards you, unlucky otherwise
If you pick sticks on Sunday you will be taken up in the moon
It is unlucky for two people to look in a mirror at the same time
Seven years' trouble ensue if a mirror is broken
Tea leaves on a cup of tea indicate visitors, a long leaf a tall person, a short leaf a short person. Place leaf in the palm and bang with fist, counting days of the week. The day for arrival is when the leaf sticks to the fist
Never keep broken cloam or combs
It is unlucky to put umbrella or shoes on the table
Burn bones and you will hear groans
It is unlucky to lend salt or borrow it
If the rooster crows in the door, visitors can be expected
Having gone out and forgotten something the person must, on returning sit on the stairs and count ten
If you knock your spoon through the bottom of the shell of a boiled egg no ill luck will befall you
If egg shells are not broken, witches will go to sea in them
Evergreens must be removed from the house before Twelfth Night. It is defying God to burn them, they must be thrown out to decay
To preserve the house from fire take branches of seaweed, dry, and fasten in turned wooden frames and stand on mantelpiece
A loaf of bread upside down indicates a row
When a convalescent person goes out for the first time he must make a circuit of the house with the sun

'As ragged as Jy weth es shirt hangin' out'.

May cats bring in snakes and adders

It is unlucky to meet on the stairs

A maid-servant who brings in a branch of hawthorn on the first of
May is entitled to a dish of cream

A hole must be left in one corner of the wall of a house for the piskies
to come in and out

Quarrels in the house will ensue if gravy is poured out of a spoon
backwards

Put on the left stocking first for good luck

If fire won't kindle your husband is in a bad temper

The fire hook and prong should be crossed to keep out witches

The brandis [trivet] should be turned down on the baking iron to
prevent the small folk sitting on it

The hearthstone should be swept and a basin of spring water left
before it for fairies to wash their babies

Wash-day rhymes – PAR

They that wash on Monday, have all the week to dry;
They that wash on Tuesday, are not so much awry;
They that wash on Wednesday, are not so much to blame;
They that wash on Thursday, wash for shame;
They that wash on Friday, wash in need,
But they that wash on Saturday, are sluts indeed

Stir with a knife, you stir up strife

House leek planted on the roof will preserve the place from
lightning

A stranger in your house on Christmas Day means bad luck in the
following year

Servants coming in a new situation on a Saturday or after mid-day
dinner do not stay long

It is unlucky to sit in the stairs, to cut butter or bread both ends, or
sit on the table

Busts or statues or other figures are poor luck to bring indoors

At St. Just on the first of March it was the custom to brush the
doorstep first thing in the morning to brush away all fleas from
the house for the ensuing year

It is unlucky to keep plants in a bedroom

It is unlucky to watch a friend go out of sight through a window

A ginger cat is a charm against fire

Mirrors should be covered when there is lightning. Doors should be left open in a thunder storm

The recipient of a knife as a gift should give the donor a halfpenny to prevent cutting the friendship

It is unlucky to sit thirteen at a table

Never start a fresh job on a Friday

Knife falls gentleman calls, fork falls lady calls, spoon falls baby calls

Bad luck will follow the spilling of salt unless some is thrown over the left shoulder

Beautiful nice like organ broth [made from organs – i.e. offal]

Wash-day rhymes – St AUSTELL
Wash on Monday for health,
Wash on Tuesday for wealth,
Wash on Wednesday, best day of all;
Wash on Thursday for crosses,
Wash on Friday for losses
Wash on Saturday, no luck at all

If you walk through a house without sitting down you will never go there again

Crossed knives are unlucky

A knife on edge indicates a row

It is unlucky to destroy a colony of ants

It is lucky to fall up the stairs

Spit on money for luck

It is unlucky to see the new moon through glass, but if outdoors turn your money and wish

If you break one thing you are sure to break three

It is lucky to hear the cuckoo for the first time on the right ear, unlucky on the left

If you drop your umbrella or gloves it is unlucky to pick them up yourself; if someone else picks them up they will get a surprise

White geraniums or white pelargoniums bring poor luck

It is unlucky to mend your own gloves. This does not apply to mending other peoples gloves

Like Lanson gaol, oal upside down – and other Cornish proverbs

'Tedn' all the world nor half a parish

Childrens' tongues will cut your throat with a bar of soap, or hang you with a yard of cotton

Clear as you go and you'll never be in a fouch [muddle]

Nuff's nuff, too much is a feast

A stew that do boil is a stew that will spoil

Towsers in one generation, towsers again in the third

Empty plates, full bellies

Good health is a merry meal

At Poldice the men are like mice

Kisses are out of season when gorse is out of bloom

Clean the corners and the middle will clean itself

Meat, money and light, all in one night [a good catch of pilchards]

'Like Jan Tresize's geese, never happy unless they be wherr they baint'.

17

Carry a knife, a piece of string and some money, you can cut, tie and buy

Do something for your meat if you get your drink for nothing

Laziness edn' wuth nawthun unless 'tes well folleyed

A change of work is a as good as a tich-pipe [a rest]

Hiding is so bad as stealing [hiding someone else's property]

A toad is a diamond in a duck's eye

Store is no sore

Forehand pay is the wust of pay

You'll live till you die like Nickety Booth

Dumb priests lose their benefits

Time and patience will wear out moor stones postes

Quietness is the best noise as Uncle Johnny said when he knocked down his wife

Come easy, go easy

The devil is good to his own

Promises are like pie crusts, made to be broken

No catch 'ee, no 'ave 'ee

An artful maid is stronger than Bolster. [The Cornish giant Bolster was tricked and killed by the artful maid St Agnes]

Everybody do know what to do with a kicking horse except he that got un

A roaring cow do soon forget her calf

Like an old sheep, always seeing greener fields farther on

The old must go, the young may go

Flowers fade on flirts

Pride is never cold

Three on one horse like going to Morvah Fair

The Lord will provide,if He doesn't He isn't to His promises

Like Lanson gaol, oal upside down

Wan behind t'other like Scazza men's ducks [Portscatho]

Like Tregonetha Fair, nigh by and handy

Everybody to their choice, like the old woman when she kissed the donkey

Turn the best side to London. [put best side out]

At work – Stiff as Barker's knee

Rise with the craw,
And go to bed with the yaw [ewe]

Graffled up like an arish pig
Fit like a mungern [straw horse collar]

A horse with one white foot, keep it not a day,
A horse with two white feet, sell it far away,
A horse with three white feet, sell it to a friend,
A horse with four white feet, keep it to the end

*'Bit by bit as the cat
said when he
swallowed the hatchet,
I'll manage it but it'll
be a tight fit'.*

No manure can beat the farmer's foot.
Coming to come like the old woman's butter [nearly finished]

If the first lambs of the season are looking towards you that is
a sign of good luck.

If the first lamb of the season is an ewe then the farmer's wife is boss
for the ensuing year and vice versa.

To ensure a good apple crop place a piece of toast in the fork of the
biggest tree in the orchard.

To remove bees on Good Friday will cause them to die
Oxen go down on their knees on Christmas Eve in an attitude of
devotion

Whistling by night is unlucky to fishermen

Fishermen would not go to sea if the vicar, minister, or Salvation Army officer came on the quay, or a woman with a cast in her eye, bad luck would ensue [This can now be counteracted by touching cold iron]

Rabbits and pigs must not be mentioned when fishermen go to sea

It is unlucky to eat pilchards from head downwards, eating from tail to head brings fish to the shore

Sunday's moon the sailor's dread

A caul [membrane in which a child is enclosed before birth] was said to be lucky to fishermen. According to an old story, at Cadgwith fishermen would give the donor of a dried caul free fish for life so that good luck would be assured

No miner would ever think of making a cross on a mine, because it might offend the knackers [little folk]. A miner named Barker in some way offended the knackers and was crippled by them, hence the saying 'As stiff as Barker's knee'

Miners who saw a snail on the way to work dropped a piece of tallow from their candles by its side, bad luck would ensue else

No whistling was allowed underground because it might upset the knackers

If you place a piece of tin in a bank of muryans [ants] at a certain stage of the moon it will turn to silver. Cornish miners believed that muryans were the 'small people' in their state of decay off the earth

If you meet a woman on the way to the pit in the middle of the night bad luck will follow

If a miner washes his back he will suffer from weakness in the back

Bad luck of the worst sort will follow a miner who turns back and re-enters his house after leaving for the pit

If you see a miner going to work speak up clearly, lest the missing of this civility should send the man to his labours out of heart. The miner might think the passer-by was an ill-wisher if he didn't

Receipts and charms for the cure of man and beastes – Medicine with a good 'seddlement' is best

Charm for toothache:
Upon a rock St Peter stood, towards Jerusalem. And Peter prayed,
Lord, forgive me my sins, and I shall be free. In the name of the
Father, and of the Son, and of the Holy Ghost, Amen.
[Say three times a day, three days running, and drink powdered
brimstone water between whiles.]
A tooth from a dead man's mouth is an infallible charm if carried in
the pocket
No more toothache for a year if a nail is driven into an oak tree or if
the first fern to appear in the Spring is bitten from the ground
Another cure is to catch a frog, open its mouth, spit into, and cast
the frog away. Pepper rubbed into the gums will allay the pain

*'Everbody to their choice
like the old woman when she
kissed the donkey'.*

To keep away evil spirits from cattle, nail four horse shoes in the
form of a cross against the door
To cure colic stand on one's head for a quarter of an hour
To cure heartache sleep with the key of the church door around your
neck

Black spiders dried and powered cure heartburn

Water taken from the church font is good for children with rickets and will straighten bow-legged children and children with the wobbles

To cure boils creep on hands and knees beneath a bramble grown into soil at both ends, or bore a hole in a nutmeg and tie round your neck and nibble nine mornings fasting and boils will disappear

Breathe over a newly made grave to cure a cough

Take a spoonful of earth from the grave of a newly interred virgin, dissolve in water, and drink fasting to cure decline [tuberculosis].

To cure a tumour place on it the hand of a man who has committed suicide

To cure shingles take blood drawn from a cat's tail and smear over the affected part

Bruise an ivy leaf and wrap round the toe to cure a corn, or tie a piece of fat bacon round it

To cure whooping cough eat a piece of cake belonging to a married couple called John and Joan, or gather nine stones from a stream, also a quart of water [not taken against the flow] make stones red hot, put in the water and bottle. Give child a wineglassful nine mornings running

Another cure – Find female donkey, three years old, draw child naked nine times over the animal's back and under its belly. Draw three spoonfuls of milk from donkey's teats, cut three hairs from back and belly and put in milk. Stand for three hours to acquire proper virture. Give child to drink and repeat process three successive mornings

At Sancreed as late as 1883 a girl with whooping cough was passed nine times under a donkey's belly from a man on one side to a woman on the other, a boy meanwhile feeding the animal with 'cribs'

A muslin bag full of spiders tied round patient's neck is also said to cure whooping cough

Children who are sick after whooping cough should run with the sheep

Children who cannot retain their water can be cured by eating roasted mice

The dead body of an adder, bruised on the wound it has made is an infallible cure for its bite

Charmers can stop bleeding. They cannot accept money, and the patient must not say thank-you. Secrets for charming can only be handed down to the opposite sex. Sometimes a cure can be effected without the charmer seeing the patient. A boy was cured of asthma by sending the charmer his vest six times. A white witch breathed, blew and muttered strange words over warts to cure them

A church key applied to a wound stops bleeding, or else cover the wound with cobwebs

The sign of a cross drawn on wood, stone, or metal and bound over a wound stops bleeding in man or beast

To cure asthma roll spider webs in a ball and swallow them

To cure warts steal a piece of meat, run it over the warts and bury it, or pick a peapod with nine peas, throw away the ninth pea, saying, 'wart, wart, dry away'. As the pea rots warts disappear. A piece of turf can also be used. Or you can take as many pebbles as you have warts and touch each wart with corresponding pebbles. Wrap stones in cloth or paper and throw away in the road, or lose them on the way to church. Whoever picks them up will have the warts. Rub warts with fasting spittle is another remedy. Never wash your hands in water an egg has been boiled in, or you'll get warts

A stye on the eye is cured by stroking nine times with a wedding ring or a Tom cat's tail

For a scald or a burn gather nine bramble leaves and put them into a vessel of clear spring water. Pass each leaf over the scald and repeat three times to each leaf, 'Three came from the east, one with fire, and two with frost, out with thee, fire, and in with thee, frost, in the name of the Father, Son, and Holy Ghost'

A baby should wear a coral necklace to ensure easy teething

Cut off cat's ear [left one] and swallow three drops of blood in a wineglass of spring water, claimed by white witch as a cure for measles

Toad's liver fried is good for rheumatism, as also are adders' tails. The adders must be killed whilst the dew is on them. A cabbage leaf wrapped round the affected part is also said to be a cure. Some folks carry a cork, potato, or nutmeg in their pocket, or a piece of mountain ash

Fair people should wash their hair in camomile liquor. The dried camomile flowers should be steeped in boiling water and strained when cool

Miners used to believe that mundic applied to a cut would cure it, and they always liked to wash an injury in water which ran through mundic ore

Bathe feet in mustard water for a cold and drink boiled cider, or whisky with hot water and sugar. Elder tea made from dried elder flowers or leaves was another cure, or drink the juice from turnip slices with sugar between

'I forgot myself'

Boiled onion placed in a stocking will cure ear-ache

Tea made from dried camomile flowers will cure an upset stomach

Drop a key inside clothing at the back to cure nose bleeding. Vinegar and honey will help cure a cough. If a fisherman cuts himself he takes a lobworm from his bait and presses it on the wound, then throws worm in water and washes cut in water

Boosening is a cure for madness, the person is immersed in water until on the point of drowning, and repeated if necessary, [associated with Altarnun]

For sciatica carry either a knuckle bone of a leg mutton, a raw
potato, a piece of lodestone or a nutmeg in a pocket, or round the
neck

Club moss is good for eye diseases. On the third day of the moon,
when crescent is seen for the first time, show it the knife to be
used for cutting the moss saying 'As Christ healed the issue of
blood, do thou cut what thou cuttest for good'. At sun-down wash
hands, kneel, cut moss, wrap it in white cloth and boil in water
from spring nearest its growth. Use for bathing eyes

To cure goitre, go before sunrise on the first day of May to the grave
of last young man buried in the churchyard, pass hand three
times from head to foot of grave and apply dew collected to part
affected

Mortals are we and subject to diseases,

We must all die, even and when God pleases,

Into the world but one way do we come,

A thousand ways from thence we are sent home

To cure hiccups wet the forefinger of the right hand with spittle and
cross the front of the left shoe three times saying the Lord's
Prayer backwards. Frightening the affected person is another
remedy

Ointment for bruises was made from bruised mallow leaves mixed
with lard, or treated by applying the convex side of a tablespooon

Apply a bread poultice to a whitlow

A few drops of nitre on a lump of sugar for curing bladder trouble.

Place a half-crown piece on a bleeding ulcer in the leg and secure it
to stop bleeding

Soak a handkerchief in vinegar and place on forehead to relieve
headache

Stand ankle in cold water for a sprain

A few drops of Friar's Balsam on a 'knub' of sugar will help a cold or
inhale same in hot water with a towel over the head

Rub a bad back with an empty bottle

Put red flannel or brown paper on the chest to relieve bronchitis.

Red flannel was always thought to contain more healing properties.

Sit on a hot cushion to cure diarrhoea

Rub butter on a bruise

Smear goose fat on a brown paper plaster for a chest cold

Uncle Jacky Hooper, of Blowing House, Redruth, cured sick cows by giving the owner a prayer, or chapter to read from Proverbs. To be read over the animal's back – charge five shillings

For curing infantile mesenteric disease children were taken to Chapel Euny Well, Sancreed, and washed on first three Wednesdays in May, then drawn through pool three times against the sun and three times on surrounding grass. People suffering from humour and wounds were also supposed to be cured here

Weakly children were bathed in Mennacuddle Well

To cure rheumatism boil a happorth of mustard in a pint of beer. An old lady said she had taken 27 quarts and it had done her a power of good

Take enough sulphur to cover a sixpence to keep the blood in order

For neuralgia put a plaster of fresh cow dung to the face

To cure a sore throat, sleep with a stocking from the left leg around your throat

To cure chilblains, dip the affected part in the charlie. [chamber pot]

'Mayor of Calenick walked two miles to fetch a horse to ride one'.

In the countryside – Stagged in the mud

Prick like a goad [spiked stick]
Goin' up like' smawk' [smoke]
Coming' down like rain
The cows got the wap [racing in hot weather]
Like old Jan Keat's 'oss, stagged in the mud
Kill a robin or a wran [wren] never prosper boy nor man
'Rabbits' should be the first word spoken on the first day of the
    month
A robin chirping mournfully means sad news
Cross a stile and a gate hardby, you'll be a widow before you die
A branch of an ash tree will keep away snakes

One magpie is a sign of anger,
Two a sign of mirth,
Three a sign of marriage,
Four a sign of birth,
Five for silver,
Six for gold,
Seven for a secret that must never be told

Another variation:
One's sorrow,
Two's mirth,
Three's a wedding,
Four's a birth,
Five's a christening,
Six a death,
Seven's heaven,
Eight is hell,
Nine the devil his-self

Blackberries should never be picked after the first of October
    because they have been spat on by the devil
Blackberry stains will not disappear while the fruit is in season
Picking dandelions was said to induce bed-wetting. The penalty was
    a mouse pasty

It is unlucky to cut an elder tree or its blossom without first asking
its permission or apologising to the spirit of the tree

A scow tree [elder] keeps away evil spirits

Where a bay tree grows the house will never have a fire

A pot of shamrock growing in the house is most unlucky

When you hear the cuckoo for the first time in spring, if it calls
twelve times in succession you will not want for bread for the rest
of the year

Good blackberry season, good herring season

To dream of fruit out of season means anger without reason

*'Kisses are out of season when the
gorse is out of bloom'.*

Pirates. trollops and cut-throats

It was once common to give the inhabitants of each town or village a nickname, frequently uncomplimentary, and often referring to some legendary event

Bude rats
Buryan boars
Cadgwith pilchards or fish guts
Camborne chawbacons
Camborne merry-geeks
Chacewater scat-ups
Duloe blues
Falmouth trollops
Gulval bulls
Hartland jackasses
Jacobstowe gentlemen
Kilkhampton church-goers
Launcells geese
Lelant badgers
Lizard onions
Lizard [Church town] rats
Ludgvan hurlers
Marhamchurch bulldogs
Market-jew crows
Morvah chick-chacks
Morvah devils
Mousehole cut-throats
Mullion gulls
Murstaw [Morwenstow] wreckers
Nancledrea rats
Newlyn buccas
Penryn shag-town
Penryn skiverdowns
Penzance scads [horse-mackerel]
Penzance pirates
Polperro gander-geese
Polperro stinkers

Polruan Russians
Poughill cuckoos
Poundstock stragglers
Redruth – three chops in a heel or, and a heel
St Agnes – hedged the cuckoo
St Ives hakes
St Leven witches
St Pinnock bone-pickers
St Just red-tailed drones
St Just fuggans
Sancras pigs
Sennen – [the name was 'too unseemly' to be printed by our
Victorian informant, but apparently it cast a slur on their
paternity!]
Stratton mice
Towednack buccas
Towednack cuckoos
Week St Mary ramblers
Whitstone [Cornwall] owls
Zennor goats

'Redruth men-crowned the
donkey'.

And on Scilly:

Bryher thorns [also 'lop-sided']
St Agnes' – Turks
St Martin's – ginnicks
St Mary's – bulldogs
Tresco caterpillars

Boscastle folk – know too much
Camborne men – tore up bellows to see where the wind came from
Mabe – made a clothes post from stone
Mousehole men – strubbed (robbed) the dead
Penryn men – took the church door and made it a ship's rudder
Redruth men – crowned the donkey
Ruan Vean men – don't know and won't be told
St Ives men – flogged the hake
In Polperro they'll say anything except their prayers, and them
    they'll whistle
St Ives, 'the town that went down on the sea-shore to get washed,
    and hadn't the strength to get back again'
Zennor, 'where the cow ate the bell rope'
Like a Lansallos treat – everybody pays for himself
All black and white like a Market-jew crow
Sennen men are slow but sure thinkers. They solemnly discussed
    their policy if war broke out between England and France. Their
    decision was in favour of England

The Mayor of Calenick walked two miles to fetch a horse to ride one
The Mayor of Falmouth thanked God when the town gaol was
    enlarged
Like the Mayor of Market-jew, sitting in his own light
The Mayor of Tregony could read print upside down and wasn't
    above being spoken to

Teach thy granny to lap ashes

Don't know and won't be told
Fine like Benbow's leeks, and tha could
    put five and thirty of they in a bacca-
    box
I don't care a cuss for the case, if only
    I'd got the fiddle, as uncle Ben said
Job had patience, but Job never had
    such a splat of black potatoes in
    his life
Teach thy granny to lap ashes
He's only fit to mould clay for a miner's
    hat
As rough as rats [of a person]
He can tell lies faster than a horse
    can gallop
He'd cut your throat with one hand and
    smooth it with another
Rather than do that, I'd shave me head and go
    east [to Bodmin gaol]
I'd rather be donkey to a sandman
There was one good stepmother and the pigs ate she
What things is made for money, as Uncle Jan Treloar said when he
    saw a monkey
There now I've ate my words and I aren't no fuller
It's a good job that wild cows have short horns
It's more like… than a horse is to grinding stone
From the nose of the bob to the bottom of the shaft die the death of a
    dumbledory [beetle]
Like on old yaw dressed up lamb-fashion
All to bruss and bruyans [fish bait and fragments]
As smutty and bad tempered as a bag of coals
Fit like a stocking on a man's nose
Looking like a stewed owl
He ed'n wurth his salt
Haud ee bal [stop talking], quietness is the best noise

'Clemmed to the marra'